AF219816

Special thanks

to Wesley Yates, Timothey Mellor and **especially Christian** Lorentzen
for editing my Denglish into proper words.
And to Ornella Simoni for the graphic design!

Index

Bibliografische Information der Deutschen Nationalbibliothek:
Die Deutsche Nationalbibliothek verzeichnet diese Publikation in der Deutschen Nationalbibliografie; detaillierte bibliografische Daten sind im Internet über http://dnb.dnb.de abrufbar.

Lektorat: Stefanie Fasora
Korrektorat: Anna Farfel

Herstellung und Verlag: BoD – Books on Demand, Norderstedt

ISBN 9783751921398

CHANGE YOUR PERSPECTIVE, CHANGE YOUR LIFE

...

WHAT IF YOU COVER

ONE HALF OF THE FACE?

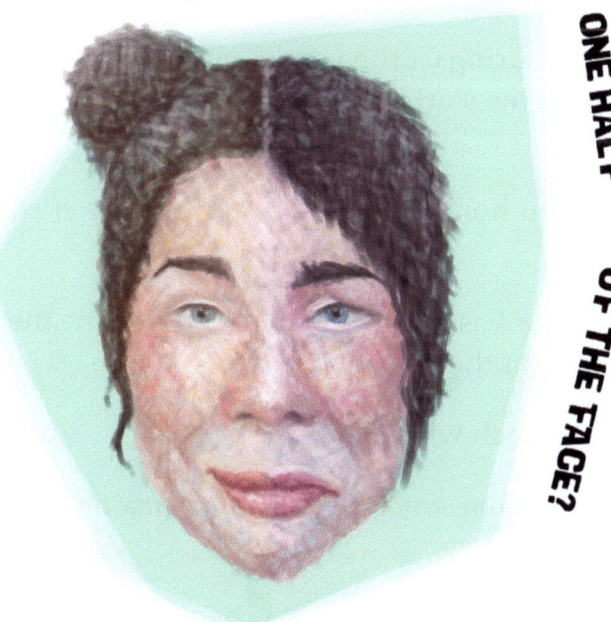

I met Anna during the Corona Crisis. I mention the word crisis, because every medal has two sides. For me this crisis was the best thing that could have happened to me. I worked on a cruise ship and when the lock down came, I got sent back to Germany, my country of origin. But two years before that, I gave all my things away, packed one suitcase and left for the world. I live where my suitcase is. So I did not have a home to go to and all my friends were in panic about the Corona and did not want to take me in. So I had to think out of the box, I contacted a farm in the middle of Bavaria and asked if they would take me in and feed me in exchange for work and help. That's were I met Anna.

It was my birthday during Corona and Anna drew this portrait for me as a gift. And that was the start of the idea to write this book and illustrate it beautifully.

Congratulations, you hold one of the beautiful side effects of COVID 19 in your hands!

My name is Stefanie Fasora and I thank you, from the bottom of my heart, that you bought this book.

You need to get in touch with me?

home.away.from.home@gmx.de

Hello world!

I am Anna Farfel, the artist, who doesn't paint. That's how I felt and I manifested it every day a bit more. Childhood injuries and adult complexes till this very moment prevented me to live my dream. I always knew that I want to paint and one day I will really do it, but … not now, that's how I procrastinated so far.

I don't think it's a coincidence that my first real painting project turned out to be this book. But I believe that meeting Stefanie was a gift from the Universe. I was illustrating this book about how to change your life and it actually changed mine. And now I can say for sure if our passion is bigger than our fears and insecurities, we will find the opportunities to make our wishes real. And the book you are holding in your hands right now is one of them.

Thank you for buying it and good luck on your own path of changes!

annafarfel.art@gmail.com

A great mind once said: Nothing changes, if nothing changes.

If we look at things, situations, people in our life the same way, applying the same judgment, emotions and perspective, there is no room for evolution.

We are stuck with the view of the prison window that only we built.

We cannot forgive others if we judge them for what they did. If we still feel the same emotions when we think of them, or if we repeat the same words, when we shame them for what they did. Even when years have passed and nothing has changed. We are still on bad terms, conflicted and troubled.

We can easily say: "Wouldn't it be nice if the world was at peace? If we could stop all war?"

If there was peace in the world, all continents would have to commit to the ideal with one another. Therefor all countries would have to be at peace with each other. Therefor all states would have to be at peace with each other, all cities, all towns, all communities, all neighbors, all people.

If we are still in conflict with our workmate, our boss, our neighbor, our stepmother, our ex-husband, we cannot expect peace in the world if we ourselves are unable to balance our own worlds in harmony.

It starts with you.

This book is about how to change your perspective, to change your emotion, to change your inner voice, how to let go of judgment and create peace on a very fundamental level.

I will use situations from my everyday life to show you examples from different perspectives, sneak peak behind the curtain. I encourage you, to also use trigger situations in your life and detach yourself from your favorite perspective and see it from another angle and how your life can change, with this knowledge.

WHEN LIFE FALLS APART

Most of us live our lives according to established and repeating routines. Days, weeks, months, and years pass by. None are too bad. None are too good. They are all, you know, in the comfort zone. Today is similar to yesterday. This week is similar to last week. This year is similar to last year. You know exactly what's going to be coming. You can rely on things. You are safe. And then BOOM, it happens. Crisis! Disease! Conflict! And nothing, really nothing, is like it was before.

When this occurs, the perspective we use is always the same, always the negative one: "Why me?" "What a punishment." "This is sooo bad!" "What did I do to deserve THIS?!"

Have you ever heard about the frog and the hot water? I want to share this experiment with you to show you how changes can occur gradually or suddenly.

First variation: You put a frog in a pot of cold water, put the pot on the stove, and heat it up gradually.

Outcome: The frog will die, because he adapts to the slow, incremental change until he's dead.

Second variation: You put the pot on the stove, heat up the water until it boils and then put the frog in.

Outcome: The frog jumps right back outside and hops away.

Many of us are in that first pot. The one where the water warms up gradually. You are in a relationship with a partner - a person you might not want to grow old with - but for the moment is ok. You're ok. You're not alone. Who needs butterflies in their stomachs anyway?

Your job pays the rent. It's not your dream job, but seriously, who on earth has fun working anyway?! It's called work, right?! Not fun. And there is always the weekend. Having two days of fun out of seven is better than not having any at all.

Your back hurts in the morning. Thank god for pharmaceuticals and pain killers, they allow you to make it through the day.

Not too bad, not too good.

And then BOOM.

Your partner breaks up with you. You get fired. A disc slips out of your spine. And things are no longer like they used to be. Not too bad, not too good.

Shit! Shit! Shit!

F*******ck.

Now some higher power switched the gradually heating pot to instant BOIL. And you jumped out of it immediately. You got ejected.

And when you are out you say: "Damn, I am not in the familiar water anymore!" and "Shit my feet are burnt!" "Why me, that's the worst thing ever happened to me!" "I want back in!" "I want everything to be like it was before." "I hate change!" Because in this moment, the moment right after you've jumped out, you do not realize, that you would have died in this pot.

Think back with honest, objective eyes. Was your life before that boiling moment just survival? Or was it about living life to the fullest? Please be honest with yourself. Instead of being sad about what you have lost, be excited about what you could gain. Instead of seeing a problem in the opportunity, see an opportunity in the problem.

Change your perspective that this is a punishment and the worst thing ever to have happened, to being grateful that the cards have been shuffled again and anything is possible now. You are a white sheet of paper. You can construct the life you want.

The question you should ask yourself every night before you go to bed is: "What's good about this?" Ask again: "What's absolutely perfect about this?" Ask yourself that question as many times as it takes for an answer to come. For an answer will come. Something good comes in every challenge.

Every coin has two sides.

Your next partner will adore you and see all your good qualities. You will enjoy the next job so much, that it does not feel like work at all, but is fun! You discover energy healing and heal the cause of the pain instead of the symptom.

We don't know what we don't know. There is an entire world full of awe out there, and thank God you are out of the boiling water now so you can see it!

BE CAREFUL WHAT YOU WISH FOR

Language is such an important part of change, that we really need to put more awareness into our words.

If you say for example "I don't want to be fat," the trigger word for the subconscious is fat. That's where the attention goes, and that's where the energy follows. "Fat" is what's being manifested. Even though it's the last thing you want! If you express what you don't want, unconsciously you manifest exactly that.

Better to flip that sentence to what you want. "I want to be skinny." The attention is on skinny and that is what you manifest.

Sounds easy enough.

But I had another idea. I expressed what I didn't want, flipped it over, and realized that I don't want that either! So I had to replace the whole concept with something new.

I said: "I hate to disappoint." The focus is on "disappoint." That is something I did. Over and over again. So I turned it into "I love to please," and was equally shocked. No! That is not what I want either!

We are not here to please others. We are here to make our own life beautiful. And with that we radiate happiness, that will make others happy, too.

Don't set yourself on fire to brighten someone else's existence! The expectations of others are the expectations of others! It has nothing to do with you, but everything to do with them.

So I changed the whole concept of disappointing and pleasing into "So long as I feel comfortable. So long as it feels good." Every time when I would have thought "I don't want to disappoint." I consciously reminded myself "So long as I feel comfortable. So long as it feels good." The result of this change was that I disappointed less and I mastered situations with ease.

I think computer programmers understand the importance of details in commands. You get one word wrong and the whole outcome is messed up.

I want to look at the statements we make about ourselves.

"My foot hurts."

And saying this is true, because it hurts, right? Yeah, but... if I repeat this sentence to all my friends, every day.. it manifests.. so how can this foot, that now is defined by my own perspective, ever stop hurting? With this sentence, I keep it in the loop.

Reason this through with me. I cannot predict the future. (If I could I wouldn't have sold the Tesla stock 600 dollars ago)

So when I say "my foot hurts" as a fact there is no possibility that this will change in the future. Because it's expressed like a fixed thing.

But since I cannot predict the future, it would be even truer to say "my foot has been hurting." As I cannot vouch for the next second or the second after that, I cannot predict the future.

And just like that, with this slight change of wording – I've opened the possibility for change in the future - my foot, that had been hurting for 2 years, stopped hurting within 3 weeks.

I want to end this chapter with some wise words by Lao Tzu:

"WATCH YOUR THOUGHTS, THEY BECOME YOUR WORDS; WATCH YOUR WORDS, THEY BECOME YOUR ACTIONS; WATCH YOUR ACTIONS, THEY BECOME YOUR HABITS; WATCH YOUR HABITS, THEY BECOME YOUR CHARACTER; WATCH YOUR CHARACTER, IT BECOMES YOUR DESTINY."

DISRESPECT

...

I got a video call from some friends just past 10:00 at night. They were in a bar and a bit intoxicated. It was quite noisy where they were calling from, so we started talking a bit louder.

About 5 minutes into our conversation I heard Julia, who lived in the next room, hammering her fists against the wall.

When I met her the following morning she said it was very disrespectful to her, that I talked so loudly after 10 pm and I should apologize.

"The world is your mirror," is a well-known saying that came to my mind. If I had to describe Julia in one word, it would also be "disrespectful."

The community I am living in consists of various nationalities and is a constant flow of people coming and going. We eat all together at a long table and our common language is English. Julia is quite often the person who starts speaking Spanish to all the other South Americans, while I am sitting in their midst not understanding the conversation. And I find her behavior disrespectful.

So, she doesn't think speaking Spanish with the other native speakers is considered disrespectful just as I don't find it disrespectful, that one time I talked loudly on a call in my room.

So I have to conclude that respect is a very subjective perception. An evaluation of a situation through my own limiting beliefs and values. If the intention of the other person wasn't disrespect, then can that person's actions be disrespectful? And if it isn't disrespectful, then what is it?

Julia had the desire for quiet and that was interrupted when I was laughing on the phone in the other room. She had the expectation that the evening would be quiet and the reality was different.

I had the need for community and togetherness. That need was difficult for me to meet, when the group is speaking a language that I do not understand. I had the expectation of a meal together with peer connection and the reality was different.

In both cases we have an unmet need and a favorite strategy to meet it.

Her strategy: The world should be quiet after 10 pm.
My strategy: everyone should speak English.

The problem with both our strategies is that they depend 100% on other people. And we cannot change the world or others (believe me, I tried…) We can only change and adapt ourselves. We project the disappointment of the failure of our favorite strategy onto the other person and call it "disrespectful".

Life would be easier, if we concentrated on our needs and found other strategies to meet it. Because demanding an apology from our own projections will in fact not get us anywhere. Quite the reverse. We expand the gap that is already between us.

So she could wear earplugs, or listen to music, use noise cancellation headphones, go for a walk, sleep in another room ...

I could talk to the remaining non-Spanish speakers on the table, learn Spanish, connect to a good conversation in my head ....
It makes life easier, if we distinguish between what our need is and what our strategy is.
A very easy example: You are hungry.
The need: Fuel.
The strategy: Burger. Alternative strategy: Pizza. Alternative strategy: Chocolate. Alternative strategy: Salad...
For every need there are thousands of strategies. You could even eat something that you don't like at all – and it would meet your need (fuel). If we are not aware of this difference, we limit ourselves in possibilities. When I know my need is fuel – I can eat anything to meet the need. When I mix up the need with the strategy and think my need is a burger I am limited to only this one solution.

The only time you run out of chances is when you stop taking them. Expand your possibilities. The world is at your service.

JULY, 4 + 11 + 13

JULY, 5 +7 +11

JULY, 6 +3 +7

TAKING ON RESPONSIBILITY

Last year, during one of the last days I had at the place in Denmark I was volunteering at, we planned a nice last evening with a bonfire, games, marshmallows and music.

Elisa, who also lives here on the estate, came to me and asked me to not play any music in the evening around the fire.

She told me that she had a car accident years ago and ever since then she cannot be around loud noises any more. She gets stressed and panics. That's why she lives here in nature, surrounded by forests, to enjoy the quiet. She gets early retirement payments from the government, as she cannot work because of her condition. But unfortunately, it's difficult for her here also, to keep us volunteers quiet, because we have new ones coming every month. After telling me all this, she stresses again: So please, no music around the fire and keep the conversations in a quiet tone.

Since I am very solution orientated, I replied "Well it's a shame, you didn't tell me earlier, I could have done hypnotherapy with you, so you can handle stress better."

To my amazement she reacted rather outraged. "Everyone here tells me what I should do." Meditation, transformational breath, and now hypnosis. She did try a lot, she said, but nothing worked. She just accepted that loud noises will always cause her stress and people should stop telling her what to do.

That got me thinking. Why is that, that people tend to tell her what to do? And then I realized, she does exactly the same: well she tells the people what not to do. (No music, no loud talking) And of course no one likes it, to be told what to do and what not to do. She doesn't, and everyone else doesn't either.

I think a little bit further: It is her problem. She gets stressed when there is loud noise around her and decided that the solution is that everyone else should (re)act differently, so that she can handle her problem better. The tricky part of this solution is: it is totally dependent on the mercy of the people around her. Of course she can ask us to be considerate and have a quiet night. But at the end of the day, she cannot influence what people are going to do or not. We cannot change the world, only ourselves. And the better solution is to take responsibility for your own problems and find solutions that you indeed can influence.

Tony Robbins teaches us that we are all able to solve our own problems. But if our subconscious mind realizes that the problem meets at least three of our emotional needs, it will hold on to the problem until we find better strategies to meet these needs.

Since Elisa reacted so strongly, I was curious to find out what was the benefit to her of holding on to such an emotional problem. Which emotional needs does that problem meet?

1. She does not have to work anymore and gets money from the government and now she is free to spend her days in nature, what she really loves.
Emotional need met: Security (financial), Freedom

2. Others are nice and considerate and do what she says and limit noise around her.
Emotion need met: Connection, Care, Significance (seriously, I would love it if everyone just does what I say, but I guess I need to have a problem to achieve that…)

3. Others listen to her problem and understand and or are trying to help:
Emotional need met: connection, significance, consideration, care

I understand why her subconscious wants to keep the problem. Those emotional needs were met. The benefits to her outweigh the inconvenience of having to be a bother.

At the same time I'm upset because I have done the active work necessary to identify my own emotional needs and find better strategies to meet them. I don't have to have my subconscious come up with problems to meet my needs. And after all of the effort I put into this active work, I do not want to behave like I have a problem. I can listen to music, I can laugh, I like when others laugh out loud around me.

And I don't think I'm being very considerate to myself, if after I put myself through all this effort to be free of problems, to live a life tiptoeing around others that do not do the work.

Every person does the best they can in every situation. Because if they could do better, they would. Once you can do better, you will not devolve. No latte-artist would make a coffee without art on top. They can, so they wouldn't go back to do nothing. And every person can find and work on better strategies to meet their needs. Strategies that are a win win for everyone.

Yes, it's work, and yes, there is the potential that the strategy fails, and yes, it takes courage. But it will evolve you into a better person and make life for yourself and others easier. The choice is yours. What person do you want to become?

Looking at Elisa again. She suffers from her problem AND the people around her suffer from restrictions. That would be a lose-lose strategy. It's like eating something you don't like. It meets the need of fuel, but it just doesn't taste good.
So what else can she do, to meet her needs for security, connection, significance, care, freedom, consideration?

What else, for example, provides certainty or security?

Have a routine, possess valuables, achieve a goal, develop skills (once you have that skill, you can be certain of it, no one can take that from you again), look into your past and realize: I have survived every single day of my life so far – no matter how hard it was. And I will manage the same in the future.

How can you meet your need for significance?

There are 2 ways to have the highest building in town – either you tear all the other buildings down, which are higher than yours, or you build the highest building. Guess which strategy is the sustainable one and which one is the destructive one…

Doing good, giving gifts (you know how significant you feel when you are on the receiving end of gratitude), master a skill, live your life to inspire others, build, create, achieve goals.

Good strategies to meet your need for connection:

Do volunteer work – connect with other volunteers, care for people, join a club, have a good circle of friends going, love someone, meditate.

Everyone finds a way to meet their needs. The question is not if, but how! Do you meet the need in a way that empowers you and helps others? Or do you meet your need in a way that harms you and others?

The choice is yours!

WHAT IS YOUR STRATEGY TO MEET THE NEED?

WHY IT IS DIFFICULT TO LET GO OF TRAUMA

Damian Richter once said:

"WE ARE THE SUM OF THE STORIES WE TELL."

What is the motivation behind telling something to someone anyway?

I think we tell our stories for reasons like gaining recognition, confirmation, comfort… Basically to have our emotional needs met through the reaction of the listener.

I wouldn't explain a cake recipe to someone who did not ask for it. They would be confused and ask me, why am I telling them this, right now? And I have no emotional need to be met in telling it to them. So I wouldn't even think of doing that. Because everything we do is done to meet our needs.

My neighbour Ulla tells me about her childhood. Bad things happened to her then. She joined several trauma therapies, but still hasn't been able to let go of it. Her therapist even said that other patients did not go through even 10% of what Ulla went through. That last part she tells me with a hint of pride in her voice. And I believe that's the crucial point.

As long as she gets recognition for telling this story, as long as she gets affirmation of her strength, as long as this trauma meets some of her emotional needs, she won't let go of it and move past it. A dog would never stop putting that puppy-eye-look on his face. Because he knows, it works. And whatever works will be kept as a tool by the subconscious mind.

But on the other hand it's a trauma, a bad experience, a thing that the conscious mind really wants to forget. So how can I let go of it?

I need to find a story to tell, that also makes me proud of myself, and that gives me recognition, comfort, confirmation, sympathy from others.

To see this trauma-narrative from a different, and very sober perspective: I am not getting recognition for what I have achieved, but rather I am getting recognition for enduring what the offender did TO me. Because trauma is experienced in the passive victim state. I am basically boasting about the deeds of others that I simply lived through.

So to let go of my trauma, I must do an assessment, what did I achieve during my life? And if I have not achieved anything more significant in my life than that trauma, well I will have to kick my ass and start doing things that make me proud. I must set goals and achieve them. Then I will be able to tell different stories I am more proud of, while still meeting the same emotional needs storytelling provides.

I actually know what I am talking about here. It is so easy to blame my own failures and short-comings on childhood traumas. Because, like most of us, I have had shitty experiences in my childhood.

I was convinced that my life was as shitty as it was, because of what my mom did. What she did. And I saw myself as the victim of this trauma can't do anything. I cannot change the past, right?!? She traumatized me for my entire life, that bitch! I cannot live my life like I want, because of HER and what SHE did to me! I was mad, I was angry with her. Even for everything that went wrong in my life when I was 30 years old, I still blamed her. Because, you know, she was the very root of my failure, she messed up! Because of what she did 25 years ago. I will suffer until the end of my life.

But if we are honest with ourselves. Who is the only person that lives my life? ME! Who decides, which stories I tell? ME. Who decides what I achieve? ME! Who is responsible for my failure? ME!

When I tell stories based on trauma, I am boasting about the deeds of others, not any of my own.

So am I ready to see that it's time to achieve something on my own? Can I tell new stories? Stories in which I am the hero not the victim.

Thanks to my mother and what she did in my childhood, I was driven! I used to own my own cafe bar, I wrote a book – even one before this one,

I was the leader of a support group, I created a meditation CD, I became a hypnotist and helped people to change their lives. I am a latte-art-artist, I managed a social housing project, I organized a festival of happiness, I reduced all my belongings to one suitcase and travelled around the world and lived my life independently and in a self-determined way.
I am 37 years old, I can go anywhere, do anything, be anyone I like.

These are the stories I tell meanwhile. The reaction of these stories meet my needs for significance, recognition, confirmation. And I am proud as hell of myself! MY achievements. The fact that I had trauma in my childhood became just so irrelevant, that I do not think about it any more nor feel the need to mention it any more.

Probably only 5 years ago, they would have engraved into my head stone: "The one with the trauma." Today I would need a bigger stone, otherwise all the things that my life is about will not fit.

So off you go, write your story, write it well and edit often! You choose what defines you – not your past and not the deeds of other people. Be your own hero! It might take a bit of bravery, but hey, enduring a trauma also did, so you already have the courage in you. You can do it!

BEHIND THE SCENES OF TRIGGER SITUATIONS

I joined a Facebook group called "Level up your life". New members were encouraged to introduce themselves and I started saying about how I moved out of Germany 2 years ago, reduced all my belongings to one suitcase and now "live" wherever my suitcase is.

A woman, that I will call Helena, commented on my post. Her comment was so interesting, so full of values, needs and reprimands, that I wanted to share it with you. She wrote:

"I assume and hope you are paying for all this by yourself? I have a colleague who also lives this alternatives lifestyle. Meanwhile she lives mainly at the expense of others, parents and so on. Her parents also pay for her travel insurance, they have worked hard their whole life. And when she changes her mind, or when she's too old for that (or when she'll be pregnant), she will come back and then the government has to pay for her. The alternative lifestyle and this I-live-my-life-stories should not be done on the expense of others! That's not acceptable."

As far as I understood from this comment, Helena herself is not financially supporting this colleague of hers. The colleague gets money from her parents and or other people (if this is the actual truth and not just an assumption). Helena is very upset, perhaps even angry about that – even though it does not affect her financially in any way. Why is that?

Also Helena predicts the future, that the colleague will get pregnant or be too old to live this kind of life and then come back to Germany to get social benefits. This scenario is one of many possibilities. It might happen that way. It also might not happen that way. What she assumed is definitely not a fact. Yet Helena is upset and angry. Even though it has not happened or might not even happen at all. Why is that?

So what's the story behind this?

Neville Goddard once said: "The world is a mirror, forever reflecting what you are doing within yourself."

Whenever we get upset and angry about things that do not actually affect us, it means that we have been subconsciously triggered by our own values and limiting beliefs. This is a nudge so we can see which of our own needs have not been met at that moment. If we are brave enough to look, that is. When we point the finger at others, our other three fingers are pointing back at us. And of course it is easier to follow this one pointy finger to blame something outside of us for our feelings, but we will be looking at the three not-so-obvious fingers pointing at us.

A great way to uncover your limiting beliefs is to turn your reprimands about others into "I" sentences.

For example she said: it is not acceptable, if this goes at the expense of others.

We turn it: I cannot accept that others pay for things I do or want to do. I need to be able to do this by myself.

Her own limiting belief: I am not allowed to take / to receive. I need to be strong. I cannot accept help.

She also said (about the parents): they have worked hard for their whole life.

We turn it: I have to work hard for my money.

Her own limiting belief: I have to work hard to live my life.

She said: meanwhile she lives mainly at the expense of others.

We turn it: I am not allowed to live at the expense of others.

Her own limiting belief: I am not allowed to take / to receive. I need to make it on my own

These are limiting beliefs that are deeply rooted in our subconscious mind. They have been planted there by us, when we were children. When we had a limited child's perspective on things, when we drew a conclusion to something that has been said – even if it was out of the context, or to something that we have seen - we saved this conclusion as "fact" in our subconscious. And so we built our whole foundation of these conclusions without ever double checking if they still apply, if they are actually true, if they help me in life or if my life could be easier if I adjusted my perspectives.

It's because of these conclusions, that may or may not be correct, that we limit our lives, our possibilities, our fun. Just remember that people concluded the world is flat and they believed it to be true for centuries. So if that trigger comes and you get angry and upset about things that don't directly affect you, say THANK YOU. Then look at which limiting beliefs it uncovers. Because now the fun begins.

Becoming aware of your limiting beliefs is the portal to understand what emotional needs we have, that are not met. And we haven´t met them, because of these limiting beliefs that we built around us like a prison cell. Our own do's and don'ts, which we concluded as children and still believe to be true. But are they? Or do they just own us and leave us in the cell?

So now let's find Helenas un-met needs within these limiting beliefs.

Need: Ease. Easiness.
Are you upset, because your colleague seems to have it so easy, while you have to work hard for your money and your life? Wouldn't it be nice if your life was easier? How can you achieve ease in YOUR life? What can you do to make your life easier?

Need: Significance / Love
Are you envious, because she seems to get so much, while you "have to" fend for yourself? Wouldn't it be nice, that someone gives you such a big

gift, because you are worth it? Because they love you?

What can you do, that you are proud of yourself and content with yourself and your life?

Need: Freedom / Variety

Are you upset, because your colleague does what she likes, while you do what's expected of you? Wouldn't it be nice if you could just live your life like you want it? If you could do whatever you like?

What can you do that brings variety into your life? What would give you more space to be you?

So the clever way of dealing with trigger situations is to let go of reprimands and meet YOUR need.

When we don't meet our emotional needs, we are not centered and we will react from trigger to trigger and this is a never ending story. We are guided by life's externalities. The moment we look within ourselves and not at the trigger, we can find our un-met needs and meet them. To become centered and act rather than react. Live our life rather than be lived by life. Trigger situations will show up less and less in your life the more balanced you are.

What you do with your life is your choice, it always has been. It is your life and you are the only person who created the prison bars behind which you live. Break them down! Re-conclude. We cannot change others, we can only work on ourselves.

Live your life and have FUN doing it.

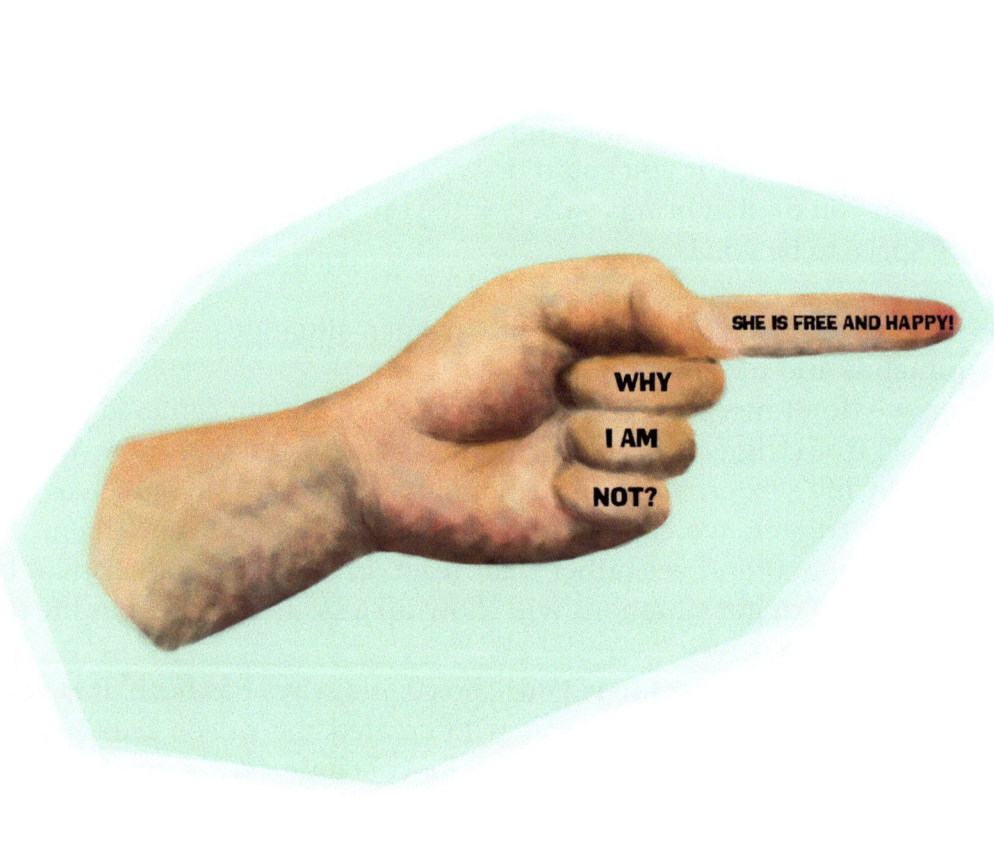

COMPROMISES

...

Around Christmas I wound up in bed with a man who was in an open relationship with another woman. He was quite forthcoming and honest about keeping his options open, which got me thinking...

Like every woman, in my utopian world, a man would be saying: "Stefanie, you are amazing, you bring out the best in me and I want to spend each and every day and night with you. I am convinced you are the best thing that ever happened to me and the last thing that I would want would be to keep my options open, because for me, there isn't anyone better than you!" That would be the respect and esteem, that I, in my own humble opinion, deserve and wish for.

And the discrepancy to what this guy was offering was huge. Elephantly huge. "Stefanie, sorry, today I am meeting with the other one, tomorrow I'll watch a movie with a new one, but on Sunday I could spend time with you again."

In the past, there would have been a voice in my head saying: "well, that's better than nothing, I guess..." But thank God, I have been working on my personal growth and evolution for six years now. Meanwhile I can - without regrets - say: "Thanks, but no thanks. That does not value me or anyone."

Let's assume I am a hypnotist and I know a bit about how the subconscious mind works. Then I would know that we draw conclusions after every experience. We make and store these conclusions in our subconscious mind as a reference point. If we have the same experience again and again, and draw the same conclusions again and again, the conclusions manifest themselves into a belief about ourselves. And according to this belief, we act in life – our conclusions become our personality.

So lets say I get involved with this guy, the one who wants to keep his options open, and he sleeps with me and at the same time he is looking for someone else (someone better?). Every time I store the same conclusion in my subconscious mind: "I am not good enough." or "I am not enough for a man.", "I cannot satisfy a man." It doesn't matter if the thought is conscious or unconscious, whether I'm even aware of it. Like learning new vocabulary, with every repetition the belief manifests itself in our subconscious - "I am not enough."

So with time my self esteem decreases and decreases until I believe in every situation (conscious or subconsciously) "I am not enough." I will stop believing in myself, in my skills, in my value. Consequently I will try out fewer new things, as I already gave up hope of being able to do anything new. So the less I try and do, of course, the less I accomplish, which would be another experience, leading to draw the conclusion "I am not enough." This is a vicious cycle that can make an emotional wreck out of any happy person, who was once full of life and confidence.

The decision to say "No thanks" is easy, if you know the consequences in advance. I cannot live two lives at the same time, right? If I live a life full of compromises, I do not have time to live the life I want! While running in the hamster wheel of compromises, I am not open for the good life, when it knocks on my door!

As children we experience situations and, while trying to understand the world, we draw assumptions and conclusions and store them as "fact" in our subconscious mind. But as children we have a very, very limited perspective. So the alleged fact might just be a very small fraction of the whole truth. But of course we do not know that as children. Our subconscious mind is a very big storage room – no information gets lost there. And whenever we feel the same feelings like in the situation, when we stored the "fact", our subconscious mind still uses this assumption, we made then, as a reference point in our adult life.

From the simple story of Snowwhite a child can draw the conclusion: "If I am pretty, I am in danger." And save the "fact": "If I am ugly, I am safe." And trust me, in my childhood, they repeated this fairytale again and again. While listening to the first part, I felt the emotions of fear, of sadness, powerlessness. Years later, as an adult, having long forgotten the conclusion that I made as a child, this "fact" is still the reference point of the subconscious.

Every time I feel the emotional cocktail of fear, sadness, or powerlessness, my subconscious checks the reference point for those feelings and comes up with the solution: "If we are ugly, we are safe.". And I'll overeat again. Stuff more Nutella down my throat. My subconscious wants to save me, so it helps to make me safe and ugly by growing pimples all over my face. Because safety is one of our core needs, it has the biggest priority in our subconscious. As long as this connection is stored in the subconscious mind, it will be the reference point for action.

So what to do now? Blame my grandparents for reading this fairytale to me? Blaming the guy who wanted to keep his options open? That's not really changing anything, is it?

I want to stress this again: It is not what happened to us, that is the trigger to our problems. Rather, it is the false conclusion we drew, storing it as a "fact" in the infinite storage room called our subconscious mind. We didn't have all the information. We didn't see the whole picture. But the good thing is, now we have the power to change it. All we need to do is to change the reference point. Hypnotherapy, Tapping, transformational breath, wingwave. Endless possibilities. The only time you run out of chances is when you stop taking them.
We cannot change the cards we were given, but we can choose how we play them. The smart player wins the game.

COCTAIL
«COMPROMISE»

FEAR

SADNESS

HELPNESSNESS

HOLDING ON TO ANGER

Buddha said:

"Holding on to anger is like drinking poison and expecting the other person to die."

When I was little, my dad cheated on my mother. She found out, got very angry, and kicked him out. Anger is the force that makes you strong. Anger gives you the "I-can-do-it!"-confidence to take action. It moves mountains. It gets things done.

But once the decision is made, the action is taken almost immediately. The guy is out of the door and his clothes followed him out the window. Now there is no need for this strong, angry force of anymore, is there?

A year later, my mother was still angry about that guy who cheated on her and ruined her perfect picture of a happy family life. 10 years later, my mother got chronic pain, and still talked about what an asshole my father is. 25 years later, I asked her one day: "Mom, do you remember, when we were kids, and when we slept over at our grandparents, in which room did we sleep?"

Her reply was: "It was all your father's fault. He sent me on holidays, and dropped you off at the grandparents, so he could fool around with this other woman! He ruined everything!"

I was stunned by her reply, that did not in the least answer my question. This anger was still so present, that it appears in full force at the slightest trigger. This emotion called anger turned into bitterness, which is not an emotion anymore, but a personality trait. Meanwhile, doctors don't know what to do anymore about her chronic pain, other than giving her morphine. Did this chronic pain manifest itself in her body because of her chronic anger?

And now, 31 (!) years later, morphine does not work for her anymore. And she still hasn't let go of the anger about my father. I wonder how her life might have been different if she had let go of this anger the moment she closed that door. She could have concentrated on making the best of HER life. Our life. Leaving the past in the past. She could have started with a new white sheet of paper. Started a new story instead of dragging my dad through her whole life.

All the time I wanted to change her. Forcefully even. To have less pain. To enjoy her life. But she is so resistant to anything alternative to painkillers. And forgiving or letting go of the anger towards my father after 3 decades is still not an option. The more I tried, the less she listened. Only this year I realized that she, exactly as she is, is actually an inspiration for people to not be like this. She helped me and Anna to understand the consequences of holding on to anger.

In seeing so clearly what we don't want to be, the solution, the motivation, the understanding was born to help us have the strength to change our own perspectives about holding on to our own anger-in-life stories. We got to see the other side of the coin, creating a pain-free and happy life. Having our own life is the gift we got and being able to decide how we want to create it. How we want to deal with situations. What is worth holding on to, and what is better to let go of.

C JoyBell C once said:

"Choose the battles you fight wisely."

Everything we do, we do to meet our own needs. Why did I want to change my mom in the first place? I guess so I would be the saviour. I would be significant. I would earn thanks and appreciation for the rest of my life, if she lived happily and pain-free thanks to ME. Wouldn't that be nice?

But then her story would not inspire other people. I need to put my ego aside. With our unmet needs and our fixed perspective comes our judgement of what's right and wrong. And we turn into forceful soldiers for the right! And what the heck do we know, when we are only able to see this one limited perspective through the lense of unfulfilled needs?

What is right and what is wrong? More and more I come to the conclusion there is no right or wrong. Everything there is, is there for a reason.

The pain my mom endures might save a lot of us from going down that same road, making the same decision to hold on instead of letting go. Inspiring us to look forward not backwards. To create our future instead of reliving our past.

So how can I let go?

To change your perspective, just keep asking the right questions: What's good about this? What is absolutely perfect about this? How can I see this situation from another perspective? What can I learn from this?

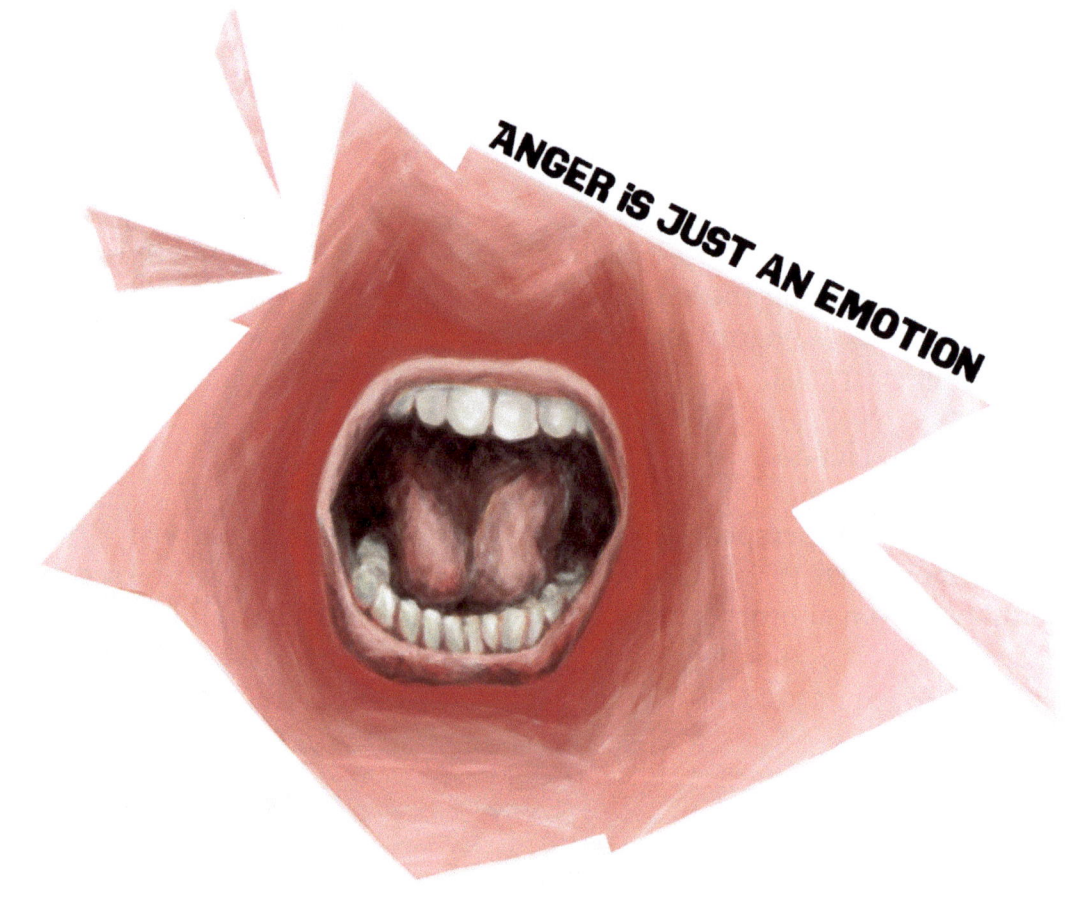

CAN WE AVOID DISEASE?

A little more than a year ago I got an email from my friend. It said:
"Dear Stefanie,
I hope you are doing better than I am. I had a brain hemorrhage and am trying to mobilize the left side of my body again."
That came as a shock.
Let's assume, it was within our power, to avoid brain hemorrhage, would you do it?

Thinking in terms of input and outcome, the action we take is the input and the consequence of that action is the outcome. So if brain hemorrhage is the consequence of something we did, we need to find out what the input was to change the outcome. Could she have done something else? What would that be? And would it change the outcome? But also consider: in order to change the outcome (I guess, that's what we all want) we need to own the responsibility for our input. Because doing the same thing and expecting a different result is the definition of insanity.

What exactly did she do until then? She is basically the Mother Theresa of Regensburg. To name one of many examples: When I had a cold, she came by with a bag full of tissues, tiger balm, and a get well soon note. She owns a holiday home that she rents out. She is the best and most considerate host I can imagine. She goes the extra mile, and then another, and another. She volunteers for various organizations, is full of sympathy and understanding, is generous, patient, and tries to bring harmony in every situation.

I have only seen her angry once in 5 years, but she apologized after every sentence for being angry.

If we watch children, they have all emotions within them: joy, sadness, anger, fear...

Our mothers raise us girls to be nice, patient, modest, quiet, friendly, considerate and adaptable. They wean off anger and rage as soon as they arise. "Girls shouldn't be angry." Is that one bullshit rule of our society? I mean, we are who we are and I do believe there is a good reason for this. Our mothers trained us to stand back and put our needs after anyone else's. Yes, they want us to fit in. They want us to have an easy life getting along with "the tribe" in society. If the world was a big jigsaw puzzle, and we all were one single piece of that puzzle, wouldn't it then be necessary that we all have our own unique shape to fit into OUR place within this puzzle?

But we were raised to fit into society, not into the puzzle, that makes this world whole. Our individual shape got so pruned and trimmed that the world's jigsaw is now full of holes. The gold we used to shine with got turned into dull metal to be like everyone else. They meant well, but that's how some limiting beliefs were planted in my friends mind: "I need to meet other people's expectations." "I must not be a burden to others." My friend is in her 60ies and I can only imagine that childhood conditioning was painfully inflicted upon her when she was a kid.

My question is: Is it possible, that something, that is a part of us, like the emotion of anger, can be weaned off? Will it dissolve in thin air?

Conditioned to suppress automatically, yes, I guess. Because my friend would say from her heart: I don't have the emotion of anger.
But as mentioned before, every child has this emotion. We just got conditioned to substitute that emotion with something more "suitable" for a girl. Sadness for example.

I explain it like this: I'm in bed, waking up in the middle of the night needing to pee. I can suppress the urge to urinate, but that does not mean that the urine is dissolved into thin air. Our entire body is one single system. And I do believe, if you suppress, suppress, suppress a strong emotion on one end, it surfaces at another end. Like an explosion. And maybe this explosion is a vein in your head causing brain hemorrhage.

Is it possible, when you constantly put yourself last by putting other people's needs before yours, you never give anger an outlet. So that one day, when the breaking point is reached, anger finds its own outlet and the body cracks with an extreme disease? A disease that changes life as you know it. Gives you a taste of the consequence, which will occur if you keep going like this. A nudge (or rather a sledgehammer) that you are on the wrong path.

And if that was true, one could avoid extreme disease, by drawing boundaries and saying "stop right there!" when someone tries to overstep them. By speaking up for yourself and putting your needs on the same level than the needs of others. By learning how to constructively express anger. By saying NO when we mean NO.

If you could avoid brain haemorrhage, would you do it? Even if it means to step out of passive victimhood and own the responsibility of the input.

YOUR WAY

...

Every morning I open a book that is filled with motivational quotes. I am always impressed how accurately it describes my situation. Yesterday I read this:

"Life is the most difficult exam. Many people fail because they try to copy others. Not realizing that everyone has a different question in front of them."

Two years ago I left Regensburg, because I wanted to live closer to the ocean. To find the perfect spot to live. I traveled along the Baltic sea, through Spain, I volunteered in Denmark, in India, I worked on a cruise ship, I helped on a farm, now I am back in Denmark… I wasn't looking for a place to stay, was I? I simply enjoyed my life.

So I am realizing now, that I assumed the idea of needing one permanent place to live from our society's ideals. That is not my question paper. I had two amazing years, and perhaps my path is just being on the path.

The world is my home. I love this sentence, because it resonates with ME.

So I invite you to think about your life. What do you do, just because "everyone does it like this". In which area of your life do you feel bored or long for something else?

Which questions are on YOUR OWN question paper?

And yes, it will take courage to change it, but it might be worth it in the end.
Imagine the day you lay on your deathbed, because we all will. Will you say: I think I missed out. I did what everyone expected of me, I need more time to live my life.
Or will you say: I created the most amazing life, I loved every second of it and now I am ready to go! Thank you!

I truly believe that fear of death decreases, when living life on your terms. On the other hand, the fear of death increases when living life according to the expectations of others and ignoring your own longings.

Your life – your choice. You are the only person who has to live it! So off you go, live before you die! Live it the way it's best for you – or not – it's still your choice.

SELF LOVE

5 easy tools to integrate into your everyday life:

If I loved myself, I wouldn't be defensive, when someone criticises me.
If I loved myself, I wouldn't feel wrong, when someone makes a jokes on my account.
If I loved myself, I would be full of love and understanding for myself and others.
If I loved myself, I would look into the mirror and be happy, and therefore influence others with happiness, who would inspire others with happiness until the entire population
"levels up" on happiness.

I truly believe, that the root of most problems in our lives, is a lack of self-love. But I also know, when I say to my partner or children: "You have to love me!" And they don't feel that, that's not going to happen, right? I don't think you can force someone to feel, what they don't feel.

So how can we generate that feeling? How can we accept and love ourselves?

I used to organize a self-love-support group and here is my top 5 tips on Self Love.

1) Stop criticizing yourself. Every time we hear criticism (especially when it comes from our inner voice) our subconscious mind logs this as evidence: "I'm not good enough."

And as the evidence stacks up we begin to believe this things about ourselves.

It took me quite a while until I actually heard the voice in my head, which criticizes me. Because I was so used to it, that I really needed to pay attention and notice it. In order to shut it down, every time I heard it, I'd repeat the sentence, but I'd make it funny.

For example, when I had to drag my heavy suitcase three flights up, the voice said: "You shouldn't have bought those five books in the charity shop!" (nag nag nag). So I repeated the sentence with a heavy German accent and I started laughing to myself. I couldn't take this criticism anymore and it lost its grip on me.

Limiting my belief telling myself "I am not good enough." Was not supported in the evidence locker any longer. It's time for a reality check, maybe?

Meanwhile I know I am good enough. Did I ever double check since childhood, since this belief started? Since then I have grown, evolved, learned and improved. So clearly that my belief is now out of date, I just forgot to update it, because I got so used to the voice keeping me from progressing leaving me feeling small.

2) Every morning I read positive Affirmations, just to have new thoughts in my head, to file new evidence in my subconscious mind.

"I am perfect, exactly as I am.", "I am worthy of love.", "Everything I do, I see through the eyes of love.", "My empathy grows day by day." You could start a new habit of writing down sentences, that resonate with you, take ideas from lyrics, you're favorite books, from what inspirational and influential people say. Keep repeating them to yourself.

3) Have you ever heard the sentence "Fake it until you make it"? The movie "Catch me, if you can" is based on the use of that amazing mental tool. I wrote an identity statement and read this out loud every morning to myself. In the beginning I thought that I was exaggerating, I felt a little embarrassed. I thought to myself, if that was in fact my statement, I would be the most amazing woman on earth. Not worried I continued, because this is one of loves qualities. To see the best in people. That is the goal of the exercise, to love ourselves more! So let's fake it until we make it.

Write down all the qualities you want to have or want aspire to be, and read them day after day after day. After a month I found more and more evidence, that this is really me, I found myself. Our subconscious mind is like Google. It searches for the answer we seek.

If I say every day "oh I am so stupid!" of course it will find evidence every day of how stupid I am. So instead, just imagine what your subconscious mind can find, if you say something like this every day:

"I am an attractive, charismatic, empathic, brave, tolerant, rich, happy visionary, power woman and lover, who inspires and motivates the people around her. Everyone loves me and is grateful that I exist. I guide myself and others to success and an independent, happy lifestyle. Enjoying my abundant life and finding the partner who supports me in being me. Because I am the best thing, that ever happened to me. Even if someone tells me I am doing something wrong, I immediately know my good intention and I am able to communicate friendly and clearly what I need and why I need it."

4) Develop a gratitude practice, for every little detail, that works in your life. Everything is there in our life at the same time. The things that work and the things that don't.
The things we like and the things we don't like. Where we place our attention, is where the energy goes and things that are fueled by energy will multiply. As our brain constantly points us in the direction of what doesn't work, make a list of everything, that works and read it in desperate times:

I am grateful, that my organs work perfectly together, I have two legs which enable me to walk through my life. I am grateful that I can move my hands, that my heart beats 100.000 times a day, and I don't even have to think about it. It even beats when I am asleep, to keep me alive! I am grateful that I can taste different flavors experiencing and tasting amazing food. I am grateful that I have ears to hear my favorite music, that YouTube is for free and I can access any song at anytime anywhere.

I am grateful that my brain is so creative and I can imagine the coolest pictures and visions, that I can mentally travel anywhere I want, without even leaving the room. I am grateful, that billions of cells in my body work together in harmony and actually know what they are doing – honestly, if they asked me what they have to do, I wouldn't even know where to start. I am grateful, that I am allowed to take this masterpiece and complex machine called my body, through life.

5) Replace fear and anger with curiosity. Ask the right questions. Imagine you are in a situation, you really don't want to be in. Instead of reacting with your usual pattern (example: being annoyed, justifying yourself, leaving, being sad, being afraid, having the feeling of not being good enough.) you can ask a question to your Google brain: "What is good about that? What can I learn from this situation? What else is possible right now? What am I waiting for? Where do I want to go? How do I get there? How do I want it? How can this have another outcome? How can I do it differently? And what if it's easy? What's the first step to the solution? In what way might this be perfect? What if it's all changeable and what if it's all a choice?"

An example: One day my colleague said to me, that he thinks I am quite arrogant. Of course I could have reacted with anger, denial, justify myself or tell him, that I find HIM bloody arrogant. But I replaced fear and anger with curiosity and I asked him instead: "What exactly did I do, that made you think that?" My colleague explained and after that we became good friends!

Last but not least I want to invite you to do a challenge:
Seeing beauty. This is your scale, to check your self-love-level. When you see another person and the first thing you notice: too fat, nose too big, eyes too narrow, too many freckles, hair too thin, too much make up, too, too, too… critic critic critic… far from love, far from self-love. Change!
Do this challenge and find something beautiful in every person you meet.
Honestly and authentically. Don't say "I like your hair" if you don't. Find something, that is beautiful, Trust me, there is something beautiful in everyone.
Remember to also look and find this in yourself, too. You are beautiful.

🔍 **SELF-LOVE** SEARCH

STEFANIE FASORA & ANNA FARFEL
CHANGE YOUR PERSPECTIVE, CHANGE YOUR LIFE